IMAGES
of America

ARLINGTON

IMAGES
of America

ARLINGTON

Richard A. Duffy

ARCADIA

First published 1997
Copyright © Richard A. Duffy, 1997

ISBN 0-7524-0851-8

Published by Arcadia Publishing,
an imprint of the Chalford Publishing Corporation,
One Washington Center, Dover, New Hampshire 03820.
Printed in Great Britain

Library of Congress Cataloging-in-Publication Data applied for

For Cup

Contents

Freeman "Brig" Young sits behind the wheel in front of "YousaY" cottage in this 1911 photograph. Young was a partner of fellow Arlingtonian Francis Thompson in the Moxie soft drink business. An avid sportsman, Young used YousaY as a private clubhouse for gatherings of his like-minded friends. Although the pergola has been replaced by a covered garage, the cottage is still quite recognizable and standing just to the north of Young's main house at 372 Mystic Street. (Society for the Preservation of New England Antiquities.)

Introduction

Rather than describe this book as the history of Arlington in images, I look upon it more as the history of images in Arlington. The over 200 compelling photographs selected for this volume reflect over a century and a half of the people, places, and events viewed as worthy of recording, collecting, and preserving for future generations.

We can now add "sharing" to the above list, for this has been a wonderful opportunity to present a great number of images that might struggle to find their place in a more traditional telling of town history. The objective here is to use words to amplify the images, instead of limiting the illustrations to those that complement the text. In so doing, more of Arlington's social, cultural, and everyday economic histories—not just the monumental and momentous—come into our awareness and appreciation.

Not that words are absolutely necessary to appreciate these images. Several possess innate interest as artifacts of early photographic processes; others are outstanding for their artistic composition; many are scenes of pure beauty, lost forever. While piquing our curiosity about the "whys" and "wherefores" of Arlington's development into the town we know today, they also become strangely evocative of our senses and sentiments, making us wonder how life "felt" for those of days long past.

In gathering and organizing the following collection, the archives of The Arlington Historical Society held the greatest treasure trove, supplemented by many essential images in the possession of Robbins Library. But it would have been too simple to rely on these sources alone to deliver an abundant array of excellent images. The development of this book led me to comb through more and less obvious sources of historic photographs in New England. I started out hoping to merely fill a gap or two in the known holdings in town, and came away with some of the most surprising and exciting images from Arlington's past. It is my delight to publicly present them for the first time here.

In the midst of preparing this book, I was especially inspired and encouraged by a colleague from the Arlington Historical Commission when I noticed her examining an historic photograph that I had brought to a hearing. As much to herself as to anyone in the room, she smiled in amazement and said, "I could just look at this forever." I hope that many of these images will lead you to feel the same way.

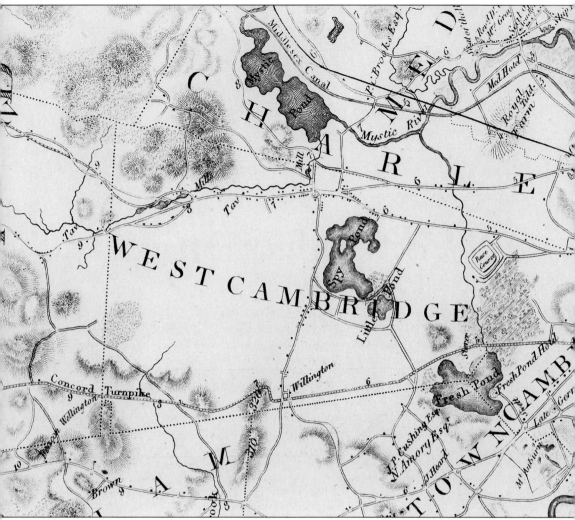

Most of the major arteries of modern-day Arlington are quite easy to locate on this 1830 map of West Cambridge and part of Charlestown by Jonathan Hales. Massachusetts Avenue, running from east to west, was the old road of Revolutionary fame to Lexington and Concord from Cambridge. In the nineteenth century, sections of it in Arlington were known variously as Main Street, High Street, or Arlington Avenue, until the entire road from Boston to Lexington was renamed Massachusetts Avenue in 1894.

Pleasant Street approaches Massachusetts Avenue from the south, and Mystic Street from the north. These later roads were cut after 1637 through the woods from Watertown and Woburn, respectively, as the routes to Captain George Cooke's water-powered gristmill—the only facility of its kind in the vicinity. Hence the expression, "all roads lead to the mill."

One
West Cambridge: 1807–1867

Arlington was first incorporated as the separate town of West Cambridge in 1807. Its legal separation from Cambridge proper preceded the dawn of practical photography by more than a quarter-century. So, beyond an early view of the center for a book about Massachusetts towns, there was apparently little that inspired contemporary artists to record life here in the early 1800s.

For most of its history as West Cambridge, Arlington was a village of under one thousand inhabitants. Its single largest employer, the Whittemore wool-card making factories, relocated to New York in 1812, thereby creating a pronounced economic slump. The continuing, but modest, success of the mills along Mill Brook, along with traditional farming, made for a slow pace of development until the 1840s, when wealthy Boston businessmen arrived to build grand "country seats" near the lakes. They would soon become year-round commuters, and actively promote interest in such matters as transportation, secondary education, and local banking. The coming of the railroad turned ice-cutting on Spy Pond into a lucrative export business, upon which West Cambridge was to largely rebuild its reputation and prosperity.

During this era, Arlington's present five square miles of territory were largely defined. To the north, the remote section of Charlestown beyond the Menotomy River (later Alewife Brook) was acquired in 1842, at the same time that Somerville was set off from it as a separate town. A portion of this new acquisition was granted to Winchester upon its creation in 1850. By far the greatest territorial loss occurred when almost all of the area south of Spy Pond was ceded to Belmont upon its incorporation in 1859. This division was a lasting source of bitterness in town, culminating in accusations decades later that Belmont was improperly refusing to construct its own almshouse, in order to pass along responsibility for the welfare of "tramps" to its mother town to the north.

This painting shows West Cambridge center in 1817. The 1804 First Parish Church is in the foreground. The Whittemore-Robbins House is shown in its original location, facing east and directly on what was then called Main Street (today's Massachusetts Avenue).

The principal herself, Miss Louisa M. Barker, made the drawing for this lithograph of what is now the Whittemore-Robbins House. The c. 1799 mansion became a girls' school for several years around 1840. Nathan Robbins, a native son who became a wealthy poultry merchant at Quincy Market, purchased the William Whittemore property in 1848.

FEMALE BOARDING SCHOOL,

AT THE

WHITTEMORE HOUSE, WEST CAMBRIDGE.

Miss LOUISA M. BARKER, Principal.

THE School Year will be divided into two Terms of twenty-two weeks : each including two quarters of eleven weeks. The Winter Term will commence on the fourth Wednesday in September, and be followed by a vacation of four weeks. The Summer Term will commence on the fourth Wednesday in March, and be succeeded by a vacation of the same length.

TERMS OF TUITION.

For full Board and the English Branches, per quarter,	$30.00
Day Scholars in Common English Studies, " "	5.00
" " " Higher English Studies, " "	7.00
For Language, in addition,	3.00
" Drawing,	3.00
" Music, with the use of the Piano,	12.00

Competent Teachers are engaged as Assistants, and more will be added to the number as the interests of the Pupils require.

The Whittemore House is pleasantly situated in the beautiful village of West Cambridge, five miles from Boston. The School room is large and pleasant, and the house commodious. Every necessary care will be taken to secure the health and happiness, as well as the moral and mental improvement of the pupils.

There being no high school in West Cambridge before 1858, it is possible that the wealthier families in town sent their daughters here as "day scholars." Note that optional instruction in music required a surcharge equal to 40% of the combined room, board, *and* tuition fees!

Reverend Thaddeus Fiske served his congregation for forty years, until they voted to embrace Unitarianism in 1828. Previously published versions of this *c.* 1850 photograph were so heavily retouched that it was believed to be a painting. This is this the first time Parson Fiske is shown bearing the features of his incredible longevity— he was the oldest clergyman in Massachusetts.

Anna Bradshaw was a key founder of the Orthodox (Pleasant Street) Congregational Church, and donated the land on which it stands. This religious group originated after losing the vote to retain Trinitarian teachings (and thus the building) at the First Parish. Similar outcomes elsewhere in Massachusetts were so acrimonious that the expression arose, "the Unitarians kept the furniture, the Orthodox kept the faith."

In 1840, the First Parish Unitarian Church constructed its third meetinghouse in the Greek Revival style. It burned to the ground only sixteen years later. Town Meeting and other government activities took place here, just as they had in the days before the separation of church and state. Hard feelings among different religious denominations, however, propelled the construction of the first town hall in 1852.

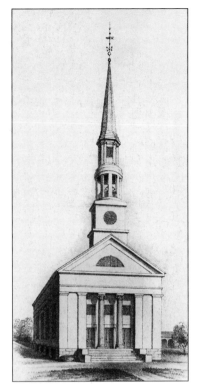

A dozen years after the split between the Orthodox Congregationalists and the Unitarians, the Universalist denomination broke away from the latter group and erected its own meetinghouse. It was moved several feet back from Massachusetts Avenue in 1860, after which there were major changes made to the front facade and tower. Today it is home to the Greek Orthodox parish of St. Athanasius the Great.

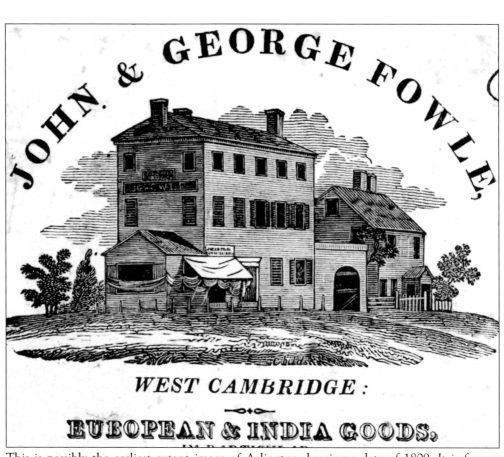

JOHN. & GEORGE FOWLE,

WEST CAMBRIDGE :

EUROPEAN & INDIA GOODS,

This is possibly the earliest extant image of Arlington, bearing a date of 1809. It is from a newspaper advertisement for the shop of John and George Fowle, which served as an early local post office and stood at the junction of the former Main and Charlestown Streets (Massachusetts Avenue and Broadway, respectively). The Civil War monument and Central Fire Station occupy the site today.

The oldest known photograph of Arlington was taken *c*. 1845. It shows what is today's junction of Massachusetts Avenue and Mystic Street shortly before the coming of the railroad. The tracks would eventually require the destruction of the Deacon Joseph Adams house (the saltbox style dwelling on the left). Previously published drawings of the house have turned out to be heavy retouchings of this primitive photographic image.

14

George Y. Wellington, a founder of The Arlington Historical Society, poses in this *c.* 1860 daguerreotype with surveyor's equipment. At the age of nineteen, he was appointed to the committee to determine the exact route of the West Cambridge and Lexington Branch Rail Road when it was first proposed in 1845. We gather that he actually assisted the hired engineers in their fieldwork.

This marvelous tintype is important for its reversed image of West Cambridge's "Town House." The image was probably taken shortly after the building's construction in 1852, making it the oldest known photograph of the building. The West Cambridge Town House was designed in brick covered with stucco (to imitate cut stone) by Boston architects Melvin & Young.

In 1851, the town fathers and volunteer firemen of West Cambridge gathered in front of the Whittemore-Robbins House to show off their newly acquired hand-pumped engine, "Eureka." This daguerreotype is reversed for publication here to show the true orientation of the south-facing gardens. The hexagonal gazebo matched the mansion's original cupola.

This rare ambrotype affords an exceptionally detailed view of Cotting Academy, a private institution acquired by the town for its first public high school in 1864. Designed in 1858 by Arlington architect/builder James Chase, it stood on a hillock above its namesake, Academy Street. The Masonic Temple now occupies the site.

Even after the steam railroad had been running through West Cambridge for thirteen years, its operations were not considered as reliable as those of the horse cars. This photograph was taken for the street railway's inaugural run in 1859. The single set of tracks was originally laid close to the side of the road, rather than down the middle of it.

With just a few days to go before starting operations, the horse railroad company announced its terms and conditions to the general public (with a special inducement for women to venture aboard). This privately run concession changed ownership at various times, but can be traced directly down to MBTA bus route #77 today.

WEST CAMBRIDGE

HORSE RAILROAD.

THE CARS WILL COMMENCE RUNNING ON

Monday, June 13th, 1859.

The time of starting will be as follows:

Leave Academy Street, West Cambridge.		Leave Bowdoin Square, Boston.	
A. M.	P. M.	A. M.	P. M.
6 20	12 20	7 20	12 20
7 20	1 20	8 20	1 20
8 20	2 20	9 20	2 20
9 20	3 20	10 20	3 20
10 20	4 20	11 20	4 20
11 20	5 20		5 20
	6 20		6 20
	7 10		7 20
	8 10		8 15
	9 10		9 15
	10 10		10 15
			11 15

THE RATES OF FARE WILL BE AS FOLLOWS:

From West Cambridge Centre to Bowdoin Square, Boston, . . . Single Fare 16 Cents, or 7 Tickets for $1.00
" Pond Street to Bowdoin Square, Boston, ... Single Fare 13 Cents, or 8 Tickets for $1.00
" West Cambridge to Mount Auburn, ... 15 Cents.
" " " " Watertown, ... 20 "
" " " " Brighton, ... 16 "
" " " " Charlestown, ... 16 "
" " " " Cambridge, ... 10 "
" " " " Porter's, ... 8 "
Within the limits of West Cambridge, the Fare will be 5 Cents.

P. S.—On the day of opening the Ladies will be carried free.

JOHN SCHOULER, } Lessees.
JESSE P. PATTEE, }

West Cambridge, June 8, 1859.

17

George Harrison Gray's homestead had a grand sloping lawn fronting on Pleasant Street, between today's Irving and Gray Streets. The original 1841 Greek Revival home was expanded and embellished with Italianate bracketing after Gray purchased it in 1846. It became home to his eldest daughter, Georgianna (Mrs. Horace H. Homer), for over six decades. The mansion was razed in 1932.

Hall's Pasture was the upper half of the Gray estate, heading west from Jason Street to about Churchill Avenue. The man in the foreground is looking down toward Massachusetts Avenue near today's Bartlett Avenue. Remains of early fieldstone boundary walls are visible in the background. Portions of these can still be seen in the vicinity of Windermere Lane.

Round Pond, a spring-fed reservoir on the Gray estate, vanished beneath the barn at Bartlett Avenue and Irving Street in 1896. It was a scenic attraction in the 1860s, with its stone retaining wall and circle of arbor vitae. Some of its water was piped down to supply the fountains of Potter's Grove on Academy Street.

This view from the porch of the Schouler mansion, which stood near the head of today's Monadnock Road, is looking toward Spy Pond. Although serenity is the theme of this stereoscopic image, the wealthy of Pleasant Street faced an annoying reality of living on the route to Brighton's slaughterhouses: cattle frequently wandered onto the beautiful moist lawns for a last meal!

Joseph S. Potter was a talented but eccentric businessman who served as state representative and led the effort to change the name of West Cambridge to Arlington in 1867. Mission accomplished, he designed an elaborate new town seal (being a talented painter of miniatures on china). He later became a state senator and then vice consul to Stuttgart, Germany.

Potter's Gothic Revival cottage residence, built at 119 Pleasant Street in 1842, had been previously the home of his father-in-law, Deacon William Adams. It was moved by George Y. Wellington to 16 Maple Street in 1874, where it stands today. Potter is whimsically posing in profile amongst the topiary hedges.

Potter developed the extraordinary Academy Street gardens known as "Potter's Grove" (one source says his own name for it was "Glenhurst"). This 1866 perspective is looking toward Massachusetts Avenue, with Cotting High School partially visible at left. The rear driveway to the M.N. Rice house at 20 Pelham Terrace once ran across the bridge, until the land below was filled for modern housing construction. (Boston Athenæum.)

The croquet lawn and its fountain can be seen on the highest levels of this Potter's Grove shot. The grounds quickly became a tourist attraction, and the public was welcome to stroll among rare species of trees and plants and a profusion of ornaments including fountains, bridges, a massive swing, and a tiered belvedere. (Boston Athenæum.)

The elegant home and grounds of John Field appear here in 1866. Field was a leather magnate in Boston. The mansion was located at today's 125 Pleasant Street, and for many years was one of the genteel boarding houses operated in the neighborhood by Mrs. M.J. Colman. It was razed in 1945. (Boston Athenæum.)

This looks like a scene from Lake Como in Italy, but is in fact an 1860s view on the grounds of the Addison Gage estate overlooking Spy Pond. Gage was an extremely successful ice merchant who owned much of the land on both sides of the pond. His mansion was moved further south on Pleasant Street in 1890 so that Addison Street could be developed for housing. It was torn down in 1957. (Boston Athenæum.)

Ridgemere, the Niles mansion at 303 Mystic Street, was one of the most elegant summer residences in West Cambridge. It was built in 1845 for Thomas J. Niles, a wealthy publisher in Boston, and later became the year-round home of his maiden daughters. The house was torn down in 1934.

The Niles estate was noted for its picturesque tower, which offered incomparable views of the Upper and Lower Mystic Lakes. Winchester's First Congregational Church steeple is in the distance. Ridgemere's 21-plus acres became the Beverly Road subdivision after World War II.

The Fred S. Squire home was a striking 1840s mansion that formerly stood on Massachusetts Avenue near Elmhurst Road in East Arlington. Like the Niles mansion, this house features the broad corner pilasters that are distinctive features of a Boston-regional variant of the Greek Revival style.

Fred's brother, John P. Squire, owned this residence at 226 Massachusetts Avenue, which is still standing as the O'Brien Funeral Home. It is shown here in its original Italianate glory, including decorative verge boards, cupola, etc. Squire's slaughterhouse and meat-packing plant in East Cambridge were among the most extensive operations of their kind in the region.

The Rodney J. Hardy residence (c. 1850) was one of the grander homes on Lake Street. Hardy's sons, happy with their own adjacent homes at 34 and 38 Gray Street, donated the estate to the town; the Hardy School was constructed here in 1925.

The history of the section of Arlington nearest the Mystic River has been greatly neglected, perhaps in part because it belonged to Charlestown until 1842. This late-eighteenth- or early-nineteenth-century dwelling once stood on Decatur Street, near its present intersection with the Mystic Valley Parkway. Notice the River Street bridge on the left, and the outhouse on the right!

The Captain Edward Russell house was a gambrel-roofed structure that pre-dated the Revolution. It stood on the site of today's Stop & Shop building.

The Jefferson Cutter House (c. 1819) is shown here on its original foundation at the site of the new Mirak Chevrolet showroom. It was moved in 1989 to its present location near Mystic Street, where it was embellished with a small historical park. Its interesting front entrance carvings have been preserved for the enjoyment of those who now know it as the Arlington Chamber of Commerce Visitor's Center.

The first brick schoolhouse in town was this simple affair, built in 1801 to serve the sparsely populated western part of town. This section of Massachusetts Avenue near the junction of Forest Street was then called High Street.

A sweetly worded invitation was drafted for a fund-raiser on behalf of Civil War soldiers to be held at the schoolhouse pictured above. Contributions were gratefully received, a dime at a time.

CHILDREN'S FESTIVAL.

Aid of the Soldiers.

The children of the North-west District will hold a Fair and Breakfast at the

OLD SCHOOL HOUSE,

On High Street, West Cambridge, on

MONDAY, MAY 2, 1864.

To which your company is respectfully invited.

THE CHILDREN.

N. B. If the weather should be stormy, it will take place the first fair day.

Admission 10 cts

There were no commercial buildings as such in the center of West Cambridge. Merchants typically occupied ordinary dwelling-houses of the period, with family quarters located above or behind the parlor or "best room." The bay windows here are as indicative of storefronts as the signs overhead. This architectural feature was not used for residences of this style until the Colonial Revival period.

The original Russell Grammar School building stood on the present site of Arlington Catholic High School. It was an Italianate, four-room structure of wood, similar to the Cutter School further to the west. It burned in 1872.

Two

Young Arlington: 1867–1889

Within five years of becoming "Arlington," the first signs of the town's ultimate destiny as a residential suburb began to appear. In the southwest section of town, previously known as Peirce's Hill, a group of investors laid out streets between Massachusetts Avenue and Park Circle, re-christening the district as Arlington Heights. The venture featured a public architecture competition for the style of home to be built in the Heights, which was prominently written about in the new weekly local, the *Arlington Advocate*. The Mount Gilboa Historic District, on the other side of Massachusetts Avenue, was largely developed during these years. Both areas are known collectively today as the Heights.

At the other extreme of town, in East Arlington, "Hendersonville" appeared at about the same time. A development project conducted by the Henderson Brothers of adjacent North Cambridge, it had the advantage of more modest prices and accessibility to the horsecar line. Nonetheless, the recession of 1875 prevented Arlington's new residential developments from meeting their targets for many years. The projects had, however, literally laid the groundwork for the shape of things to come.

The major preoccupation of the town for the rest of the century would be the water supply. The initial attempts to address this would be made in this era. First, a reservoir was constructed off Lowell Street in 1872 to hold the waters of the Great Meadows Reservation in Lexington, which were then piped into the lower sections of Arlington by means of an economical, gravity-fed system. Optimism about the system's capabilities knew no bounds: one town report predicted that the installation of hydrants would altogether replace the need for a fire department! Instead, the town water system was a fiasco. It required expensive and frequent maintenance, and the water quality was poor—engineers had neglected to remove enough of the soil before filling the reservoir. Worst of all, water would still have to be pumped into standpipes if residents in the elevated sections of town were to ever drink a drop.

The second Russell School (1873) was a far cry from its predecessor. Stylistically, it was perhaps the most extravagant non-residential structure in town—a wonderful example of high Victorian style. Only its lower two floors survive today; they were incorporated into the new Arlington Catholic High School building in 1960.

The Arlington Five Cents Savings Bank at Massachusetts Avenue and Pleasant Street was the first brick business block in town. Its construction in 1874 represented a turning point in the appearance of the center. All of Arlington's banks once had their "rooms" here. Shorn of its decorative roofline in the 1920s, it was torn down altogether in 1956.

The steeple of the Pleasant Street Congregational Church blew down in a severe 1871 gale. The skyline of almost every large New England town was once punctuated by a profusion of church spires, but after repeated losses to hurricanes and fires, steeples became more diminutive or were eliminated altogether in new building designs.

St. John's Episcopal Church was constructed in the Gothic Stick style in 1875. This photograph shows the building on its original wood foundation, at grade level with Academy and Maple Streets. In 1892 the structure was substantially raised on a brick foundation after a proper cellar was dug. Since the 1930s it has been home to the Arlington Friends of the Drama.

The first house of worship for Roman Catholics in Arlington was St. Malachy's, built in 1870 at the corner of Medford and Chestnut Streets. Begun as a mission church of St. Peter's in Cambridge, it became a full-fledged parish by 1873. It was enlarged and rededicated in honor of St. Agnes in 1900.

Father Joseph Finotti was the first permanent pastor of St. Malachy's, serving from 1873 until 1876. Given that nearly every Catholic in town was of Irish descent, it is interesting that an Italian-born priest was assigned as pastor. His whiskers were quite stylish for a man of the cloth!

Members of the Menotomy Base Ball Club posed for this picture in 1873, back when neckties were part of the uniform. Members were the sons of the Yankee establishment in town, and it is said that one of the rules in their book read: "We shall play no Irish teams."

Mike Burns was a member of what one wag termed Arlington's "Irish aristocracy" of the late nineteenth century. From the look of his enormous hands, the Menotomy Base Ball Club would have done well to welcome this Schouler Court teamster to play for them—he wouldn't have needed a glove!

The original boathouse of the Arlington Yacht (later Boat) Club was built at the end of Spring Valley in 1871. A larger facility was built at the foot of Wellington Street in 1882. Note the vegetable field on author John Townsend Trowbridge's estate to the left.

Omar Whittemore and Jim Poland make an overnight camping excursion to Elizabeth Island in Spy Pond.

Even the dog is interested in the photographer's subject, somewhere out in the hills of Arlington. This elaborate set up was necessary to obtain almost any kind of photograph in the days before higher-speed roll films.

The Arlington Lawn Tennis Club was founded in 1883 when tennis was a comparatively new game in the United States. It was a rather genteel sport at first, adopted by the croquet-playing set from the neighboring estates on Pleasant Street.

Members of the Arlington Heights Rifle Club participated in a competitive shoot in 1883. Glass-ball shooting was a popular sport in town; even the Arlington Boat Club leased land at the rear of Mount Pleasant Cemetery for use as a practice range.

Originally known as Mount Gilboa station, the Arlington Heights railroad depot was a critical element in the initial development of that area in 1872. It would be nearly twenty-five years before trolley car service would be extended from the center into the Heights.

VIEWS FROM MOUNTAINS TO THE SEA

NOTED FOR OZONE

UNRIVALLED FOR HEALTH

The Outlook, Arlington Heights, Mass.   Seven Miles from Boston.   Altitude, 373 feet

OPEN ALL THE YEAR

The Outlook, "Noted for Ozone," was built in 1874 at the northeasterly corner of Eastern Avenue and Park Circle. It was one of several spa hotels to which Bostonians would flock in the summer months.

Ring's Sanitorium and Hospital at 163 Hillside Avenue was originally built as a resort (Joel Barnard's Hotel) around 1875. Dr. Alan Mott Ring acquired it as a medical facility in 1888. His son and daughter-in-law, Doctors Frank and Barbara Ring, ran it as an exclusively psychiatric hospital. Still later a nursing home, it was razed in 1985.

A second wave of development in the Heights during the 1880s and 1890s attracted such prominent personalities as *Boston Globe* editor Edward F. Burns, who owned this home at 77 Oakland Avenue.

A rare glimpse into the private spaces of a Victorian home is afforded in this photograph. This is clearly one of the gentlemen's bedrooms at 77 Oakland, as evidenced by the stacks of starched collars and cuffs on the dresser. These detachable items would be laundered more frequently than the body of the shirt!

This cheerful wooden structure was built in 1885 as the Union Church (a non-denominational Protestant house of worship). Formally transferred to the Park Avenue Congregational Church in 1899, it was razed in the 1960s to make way for an austere brick replacement at the corner of Paul Revere Road.

This interesting view of Massachusetts Avenue in 1885 looks east toward Cambridge. The steeple is that of the old First Baptist Church, built in 1853. The car lot of the Hodgdon-Noyes Buick dealership occupies the sites of the homes in the foreground.

The Jason Russell Farmhouse (built c. 1680, enlarged in 1740) is Arlington's most important shrine to the American Revolution. Indeed, on April 19, 1775, Paul Revere passed by in the early hours warning, "The British are coming! The British are coming!" And yet it was not until Lord Percy's retreat from Lexington and Concord that afternoon that the greatest loss of life that day would occur at the Battle of Menotomy, as the then-Second Precinct of Cambridge was commonly known. After a failed ambush on the British regulars, Jason Russell and eleven others were pursued inside the house and slain there. The kitchen is said to have been ankle-deep in the blood of the patriots, and to this day several bullet holes can be seen in the house.

The house was occupied by descendants of Jason Russell until its 1923 purchase for the headquarters of The Arlington Historical Society. Today it is open to the public, offering a unique perspective on the events of 1775 in the environment of a typical farmer's dwelling of the era. The adjacent George A. Smith Museum, opened in 1980, displays exhibits covering many dimensions of Arlington history.

This photomechanical image was published in 1885, one year after Lydia Teel, a granddaughter of Jason Russell, subdivided her long-abandoned orchard into house lots and created lower Jason Street. Consequently, the most historic house in town spent most of the last one hundred years hemmed in by later structures. These were removed in time for the American Bicentennial observances, and the grounds were generally restored to their previous appearance.

The Stephen Cutter house stood diagonally across from Jason Russell's. It was plundered by the British of a year's supply of candles and a fire was set in one of its closets, but it survived to later become the residence of architect/builder James Chase. His son, Fred M. Chase, razed it to build the Colonial Garage, a predecessor of Time Oldsmobile.

They neglected to add "carrying fourteen wounds to his grave." This marker originally stood in Russell Park; St. Agnes Church is in the background. It was one of several erected around town in 1878, a lasting by-product of the enthusiasm generated by the centennial celebrations of the American Revolution.

This unusual view of the Arlington House Hotel, which stood at the corner of Massachusetts Avenue and Medford Street, shows guests at the second-floor window and its stables and outbuildings to the rear. It was actually built in 1826, but the "1775 Cooper Tavern" was added in 1875 to both sides of the building, to capitalize on centennial sentiment for the site of another massacre by the British. This photograph was taken in 1906. (Boston Public Library.)

This photograph was taken on the day the Civil War monument at Massachusetts Avenue and Broadway was dedicated in 1887. The recent addition of outdoor café seating at nearby establishments once again enables admiration of this handsome memorial, which is otherwise easily ignored by motorists at this busy junction.

This view of the new (1883) Arlington Center train depot looks southeast. It was an elaborate affair, with generous platform overhangs, bracketing under the eaves, decorative woodwork (owl's eyes?) in the gable peaks, and filigree ironwork at the roof ridges. It later became the VFW hall, and was demolished for parking spaces in the 1970s despite valiant preservation efforts.

Advocate editor and publisher Charles Symmes Parker stands with daughter Grace and son Edgar at the newspaper's offices in the old Swan's Block (today's 452–456 block of Massachusetts Avenue). The local paper first appeared December 16, 1871, and has been published weekly since 1872.

This Bracketed Italianate home was built in 1855 on grounds sloping down to Mystic Street. A modern house now occupies this frontage, so the older dwelling bears an 8 College Avenue address. It was known for many years as the Spurr Estate, having been purchased in 1885 by Boston merchant Howard S. Spurr, whose family is shown here. (Society for the Preservation of New England Antiquities.)

This intimate scene took place on the porch of the Spurr house. Notice the pince-nez eyeglasses hanging from a chain on the woman's dress. The young man is nattily outfitted for a game of tennis, a sport that was quite the craze in Arlington when this picture was made. (Society for the Preservation of New England Antiquities.)

This rustic gazebo stood on land above the rear of the Spurr house, and afforded wonderful views of the Mystic Lakes. The woman and girl are looking north toward Winchester. The mansion visible in the distance to the left of the tree was Point of Rocks, on West Medford's Brooks Estate. (Society for the Preservation of New England Antiquities.)

Since it was quite the fashion for little boys to wear long ringlets in the 1880s, it is surprising to see this little Spurr girl in such a closely cropped hairstyle. She looks every inch the young lady-in-training to become mistress of her own gracious home someday. (Society for the Preservation of New England Antiquities.)

In 1887, the year of his election as lieutenant governor of Massachusetts, John Quincy Adams Brackett (1850–1923) built this imposing Shingle-style residence at 87 Pleasant Street. In recent years it was home to the Visiting Nurses Association, before opening as An American Bed & Breakfast in 1996. Handsomely restored inside, its original exterior design may also be revived someday.

FOR

GOVERNOR,

J. Q. A. BRACKETT.

This ribbon from Brackett's 1889 election campaign portrays the young Temperance ("No-License") candidate with an appropriately stern demeanor.

Former Governor Brackett poses with his family on the front porch of his home in this *c.* 1894 cyanotype (blue-tinted) print. Daughter Minnie is squirming in the high chair next to her mother, the former Angie Peck. Brother Gaylord is having slightly greater success at holding still for the camera.

The Orthodox (Pleasant Street) Congregational Church installed an imposing new steeple to replace the one blown down in 1871. The 1844 church building is the oldest in town to be continuously occupied by the same religious denomination. Its former parsonage is to the right. It was razed to build the New England Telephone exchange in the 1950s. (Society for the Preservation of New England Antiquities.)

It is rare to see a Victorian-era pose as relaxed as this one, particularly because the image features a father and his young children. George O. Russell and his daughters Pauline and Eleanor are enjoying the backyard of their home at 28 Jason Street. The successful insurance agent later moved his family to 55 Jason Street.

By the late 1880s, the home of the Edward T. Hornblower family (of the Hornblower & Weeks stock brokerage firm) had filled in a corner of Potter's Grove. Although the little bridge shown here and a decorative roof tower have disappeared over the years, the house is still a very handsome one at 28 Academy Street. (Society for the Preservation of New England Antiquities.)

Three

Making Strides: The 1890s

In the 1890s, whatever fitfulness had characterized Arlington's growth in the preceding two decades quickly faded from memory. Horse cars had recently been replaced by electric trolleys, double tracks were laid, and service was extended to the Heights by mid-decade. Arlington eventually became a true suburban transportation hub, once Mystic Street service was established to Winchester and beyond in 1897. The tracks connected at Arlington Center for Massachusetts Avenue service to Cambridge, Broadway service to Somerville, and Medford Street service to that town. Pleasant Street was perhaps too gracious a thoroughfare to tolerate the laying of trolley car tracks and the unsightliness of "overhead electric motive power."

Where the electric cars went, new residents were not far behind. The streets of the Heights quickly filled in with houses, now that commuters had more options than the steam railroad, and soon there was no longer any need for horse-drawn barges to make Sunday runs from the Heights to Arlington Center for the church-goers of particular Christian denominations.

Arlington Center underwent profound changes. The best-recorded of these was the moving of the Whittemore-Robbins House back from the avenue and turning it to face north in 1890. Robbins Library would occupy its former site and orientation in 1892. It was undoubtedly the finest facility of its kind among neighboring towns, and strongly influenced the design of several substantial commercial buildings that would be erected in Arlington over the next few years.

It is significant that The Arlington Historical Society was organized during this decade, which was one of unprecedented speed in the old giving way to the new. The society was established in 1897 "for the gathering and recording of knowledge of the history of Arlington, and of individuals and families connected with the town; and the collection and preservation of printed and manuscript matter, and other articles of historical and antiquarian interest." These important initiatives are in many ways responsible for this book, published exactly one century after the society's founding.

The Italianate-style fourth meetinghouse of the First Parish Unitarian Church (1857), with Robbins Library at its side, filled the most dignified view of Arlington Center in the 1890s. The church was the grandest landmark in town until it burned in March of 1975—just weeks before the much-anticipated opening celebrations of the American Bicentennial.

While the proximity of Robbins Library makes it the focal point of this 1897 photograph, the background images are of greater historical interest. The long, low building in the middle ground once housed the horse cars when the street railway's terminus was at Academy Street, by the old Cotting-Pattee bakery. Single-family homes were still predominant along Massachusetts Avenue. The spires belong to the Universalist and Baptist churches.

Jesse Pattee's former home was adjacent to his bakery at the easterly corner of Academy Street. It was razed in 1906 to allow the construction of the present town hall seven years later. The front gate and sections of the fence were subsequently transplanted to the Maple Street pathway to the Whittemore-Robbins House. In recent years, local preservationists arranged for the handsome original ironwork to be faithfully reproduced.

Standing on Massachusetts Avenue near Academy Street was the old Cotting Bakery. This historic site later became known as Menotomy Hall. It once housed the fire engine "Eureka" in a ground-level annex, and above, the rooms of the Hiram Lodge of Masons, who are celebrating their centennial in this 1897 image.

The main reading room at Robbins Library is the focus of this *c.* 1892 image. The chandeliers provided lighting by both electricity (through the pointed, pendant-like glass shades) and gas (via the open, oval shades resting in brackets).

The portrait of Eli Robbins, in whose memory his wife Maria donated the funds to build the library, looks down over the rather tightly secured circulation desk.

With automobiles still in their infancy, the only difficulty in sledding down the middle of Wollaston Avenue at the turn of the century was trudging back to the top of the hill for the next run.

These members of the Arlington Boat Club pose as the proud winners of the New England four-oared shell race on Labor Day in 1893.

The second meetinghouse of the Baptists was built in 1790 at the site of Brattle Pharmacy on Massachusetts Avenue, conveniently close to Cutter's mill pond (where the ordinance of adult baptism took place). One hundred years later, the church had become a two-family home. Around 1924 the building was moved back to number 3–5 Brattle Street, where it faces west today.

Foot of the Rocks Arl.

The "Foot of the Rocks" at the junction of Massachusetts Avenue and Lowell Street was so named by farmers from western towns; the most difficult stretch of their journey to Boston markets ended here. The marker is historically noted as the scene of the first skirmish at Menotomy on April 19, 1775.

The Arlington Heights station and the West End Street Railway's trolley car barns (as the predecessors to today's MBTA garages were known) are featured in this postcard. The view certainly gave Moxie its advertising dollar's worth.

This image provides a closer view of the car barns at the Heights station. This was the terminus for trolley travel on Massachusetts Avenue until the Lexington Street Railway Company established connecting service in 1900.

The original Park Circle standpipe was erected to supply high-service water to the Heights in 1895. The standpipe addressed water quantity problems, but the water quality troubles would not be resolved until Arlington joined the Metropolitan District System in 1899.

The Crescent Hill area of Arlington Heights was a close-knit and active neighborhood right from the beginning. It had its own social association (complete with clubhouse), was active in efforts to preserve Mount Gilboa as a public park (finally rewarded a century later), and was home to this photogenic fife and drum corps.

Idahurst, located at 53 Appleton Street, was built in 1894 by Elbridge Farmer, who died just weeks before its completion. The grand mansion "enjoyed" the distinction of having the highest real estate tax assessment for a private residence in Arlington. The barn and gardens have vanished, but the house was recently rehabilitated into condominium units.

The turreted structure to the rear of this view is the oldest and only surviving portion of the Robbins Spring Hotel at 90 Robbins Road. Opened in 1898 as the Robbins Spring Nest, it won full-fledged resort hotel status with the opening of the massive, gambrel-roofed "Annex" in 1899. It housed Marycliff Academy from 1913 to 1948.

Workers prepared the pipe beds and roads of Kensington Park in 1896. This neighborhood on the former Lewis and Colbert lands was developed and named by a group of Cambridge businessmen who came to live there in some of Arlington's finest homes of the era.

This grand residence nestled in the hills of Kensington Park was typical of those first constructed in the neighborhood. By 1912, it was operated as a genteel convalescent home called Bonnyview.

The Robbins sisters—Ida, Eliza, and Caira—are icons of Arlington history. They were granddaughters of Nathan Robbins, whose family mansion, the Whittemore-Robbins House, was donated to the town in 1931. This was but part of what would be a fifty-year tradition of civic philanthropy conducted by many branches of the Robbins family.

Dr. George F. Grant is shown here in his 1870 Harvard Dental School graduation photograph. He later became the school's first black instructor, while maintaining a private practice on Charles Street in Boston. While a resident of Hillside Avenue in Arlington Heights, he is credited with having invented the golf tee in the late 1890s. (Countway Library of Medicine.)

59

This Medford Street bridge replaced a wooden one in 1893. The picture was taken at "high tide"; the waters of the Atlantic made their way into the Lower Mystic Lake twice daily until the 1906 Cradock Dam excluded them at Medford Square.

An end-of-the-century beefcake pose—at Spy Pond!

Out for a bumpy bicycle excursion—the streets were not yet paved—this turn-of-the-century trio poses in front of the *c.* 1830 Hornblower house, still standing at 200 Pleasant Street.

This festive gathering was entitled "Old Maids Party" by Miss Edith Winn, at whose family homestead, 57 Summer Street, this photograph was taken in the late 1890s. (Miss Winn was only a "young maid" at the time, and is not among this group.) Even the caterers and hired musicians, seen at left, had to be members of the spinsterhood!

61

The former high school building to the rear of the current town hall was designed by Hartwell and Richardson and opened in 1894. It became the campus for the Central Junior High when the high school moved to its present location in 1914. Multiple services for senior citizens are currently housed in this building.

One of the kindergarten classes at the Misses Wellington's School is shown here in 1898. A new school building known as Pleasant Hall was opened in 1897 at 14 Maple Street. The Gay and Proctor-designed building was converted to a private residence in 1910.

Residential delivery of the U.S. Mail was inaugurated in Arlington in 1897. Nearly silhouetted in this photograph (and having to make his way across wooden-plank sidewalks!) is an early letter carrier.

This interesting *c.* 1899 view depicts Mill Street as it intersects Massachusetts Avenue, jogging slightly to the left to meet Jason Street. The Jason Russell Farmhouse (center right) is hemmed in by the imposing dwelling since removed from the corner of its front lawn. Number 6 Mill Street is the only other structure remaining from this scene today.

Omar Whittemore's original pharmacy building takes a rest in 1896 as it heads west from its first home at the corner of Massachusetts Avenue and Medford Street. In the days before power tools, it was cheaper to move even the most humble of structures than to build anew from the ground up.

The Grand Army of the Republic (GAR) was an organization for Union veterans of the Civil War. After many years of fund-raising, the group erected this meeting hall in 1894. Most of the building's original architectural charm has been lost in its current incarnation as the American Legion Hall.

The many architectural designs of William Proctor, shown here as a young man just returned from a European study tour, have had a lasting effect on the character of Arlington. A partner in the Boston firm of Gay and Proctor, he resided at 8 Avon Place with his wife, the former Mary Spurr of Mystic Street.

Fowle's Block (1896), still standing at 444 Massachusetts Avenue, was arguably Arlington's most elegant commercial structure. Its Italian Renaissance facade by Gay and Proctor was drastically altered when Shattuck's Hardware store took over the premises in the 1930s. Even that Art Moderne renovation has since been given over to contemporary signage. (Boston Public Library.)

Looking east in 1899, this view shows Massachusetts Avenue and Water Street. Hutchinson's market, an early grocery chain, occupied this historic Thomas Russell store—said to be the oldest grocery store in New England.

This wooden commercial building was literally wrapped around the "Squire" Whittemore house at the former intersection of Mystic Street and Massachusetts Avenue. Note the three pharmacies competing all in a row. Also note the old-style barber pole above the mortar and pestle of Charles Clark's apothecary.

This view approaches the Finance Block from Medford Street. Shattuck's Hardware is the third store from the right.

This splendid 1897 view was taken to the southwest of the preceding one. It shows the former junction of Mystic Street and Massachusetts Avenue in the middle ground, and displays the relative positions of the other major structures in Arlington Center.

Daniel Ahern is fairly bursting with pride in his foreman's uniform from the Arlington Veteran Firemen's Association.

The venerable Eureka is being led westbound on Massachusetts Avenue, probably on its way back from the 1899 Patriot's Day parade.

Four

Industry and Agriculture

Although the general organization of this book is chronological, it seemed essential to dedicate a topical chapter to the town's agricultural and industrial past. It is particularly important to present these subjects in undiluted form because their history is so much less visible today than many other aspects of Arlington's built and natural environments.

Milling along the aptly named Mill Brook dates back to 1637, when Captain George Cooke established the area's first gristmill near today's Russell and Mystic Streets. The engines of Arlington's early industries were colloquially said to run on "peat tea," because the headwaters of the brook are located in the bogs of the Great Meadows Reservation. The drop in elevation from Arlington Heights to the Lower Mystic Lake enabled the little stream to flow at a rate that easily kept a two-mile chain of mill ponds filled—powering businesses as diverse as shoemaking, calico printing, saw making, wood turning, paint grinding, and grain-meal production. These small, family-owned mills were among the hundreds of thousands that employed untold numbers of European immigrants who thus found their first toehold on the ladder of social and economic success in America.

Ice cutting was as profitable as it was picturesque, and Spy Pond was reputed to yield a harvest of up to 60,000 tons in a good season. The enormous icehouses were designed to store an entire year's supply in advance, lest a warm winter disappoint major clients. By providing jobs to farm workers who would otherwise be idled in the coldest months, the economic benefits of the ice industry were widespread.

Market gardening, the raising of fresh produce for consumption in the local region, operated on such a huge scale in town that it was often referred to as industry rather than agriculture. This success owed less to the mediocre soil than it did to the practice of forcing fruits and vegetables to grow in glass hothouses, of which Arlington was once said to boast the greatest density per square mile in America. Local produce was typically the first to market each season, and Warren W. Rawson's line of seeds included several varieties that proudly bore the Arlington name.

With an abandoned millstone to mark the spot, this postcard depicts the site of the original privilege granted on Mill Brook to Captain George Cooke in 1637. His corn-grinding operation was the only one for miles around. A variety of mills operated at this site for nearly three hundred years.

The original Fowle's Grain Mills was photographed c. 1875. In 1863 Samuel A. Fowle obtained the mill from his father-in-law, Benjamin Cutter, on the site of Captain Cooke's original 1637 mill privilege. Fowle's diverse activities also included paint, dye, and drug grinding. He built an even larger mill complex after a disastrous 1883 fire, where his famous "Arlington Wheat Meal" was produced.

In 1864, German immigrant Charles Schwamb acquired a two-hundred-year-old former grist,- saw, and spice mill and converted it for the manufacture of curved and linear picture frame molding. The tremendous popularity of formal portrait photography in the late nineteenth century provided a rapidly growing market for the oval frames that were Charles Schwamb's specialty.

Charles Schwamb's oval and circular picture frames became especially popular after the Civil War. To accommodate new machinery and staff, he twice added ells to the main building. A group of employees poses with product samples in 1873, the same year that the third floor addition was built. The "mill race," through which the waterpower entered the building, is to the far right.

This 1878 photograph shows, from left, the interconnected lumber dry house, storage barn, and main manufacturing building of the Charles Schwamb Mill. After the Arlington Reservoir was built in 1872, the flow of Mill Brook was disrupted to the point that mill owners had to turn to steam engine power (and the town had to make large cash settlements to them for economic damages). Despite this changeover, the mill pond remained critical to operations. There being

as yet no town water supplied to the neighborhood, the boiler had to be filled each day with "peat tea" to generate the steam. The pond is now gone, but the mill remains. In 1969, visionary conservationists recognized it as an historic industrial artifact with unique educational value and rescued the mill from certain demolition. It is listed in the National Register of Historic Places as The Old Schwamb Mill.

The home of Theodore Schwamb, brother of Charles, is a *c.* 1850 structure still standing at 1171 Massachusetts Avenue. It has been beautifully restored (minus the porch) in recent years as law offices.

Theodore Schwamb's orchard was adjacent to his home. The mill complex visible through the trees gave a bucolic air to this early industrial area. A new Mirak Hyundai showroom has recently replaced the abandoned Citgo station that occupied this site for many years.

Theodore Schwamb owned the next mill privilege downstream from his brother Charles. A sample of his piano case product line is being transported to Arlington's 1907 Centennial Parade by this bowler-hatted quartet. When radios and phonographs supplanted the piano for home entertainment, the Theodore Schwamb Co. turned to architectural millwork. The firm was in operation until the 1960s.

An 1880 advertising card commemorates the establishment of the Welch & Griffith's saw-making factory at a Boston tide mill in 1830. Prior to that, saws were imported from Britain. Welch & Griffith's sales office remained in the city, but their factory relocated to the Mill Brook in West Cambridge in 1832, where it remained for over fifty years.

Two *c.* 1875 photographs were assembled to create this panoramic view of Welch & Griffith's saw-making factory on Grove Street. Notice the small and large mill stones near the buildings

of the left photograph. The Arlington Gas Light Company later built its handsome brick plant on this site, which is home today to the Arlington Department of Public Works.

The Cyrus Cutter mill is reflected in the pond created by the second-oldest (1704) dam privilege on Mill Brook. The old Mill Street bridge is to the right. The pond was filled in to create the playing fields behind Arlington High School.

It is easy to romanticize the market-garden era as one of simplicity and purity, but Arlington's agricultural success was due in great measure to products such as those provided by Frost's, which once occupied 22 Mill Street on the site of the Cyrus Cutter mill. The building houses office suites today.

This 1858 illustration in *Ballou's Pictorial* depicts the Addison Gage Company's ice cutters at work on Spy Pond. A branch of the Fitchburg main line that was known as the "ice railroad" carried the sawdust-packed product to the docks at Charlestown for shipment around the world.

As a young boy living near the foot of Gray Street in the early years of this century, Parry Reich recalled the operatic singing of Italian ice cutters on Spy Pond, and phonetically expressed the accents of their non-musical colleagues who implored, "No seeeng! Poosh, poosh!"

Spy Pond was not only famous for ice harvesting, but also for manufacturing many specialized tools to accomplish the job. William T. Wood purchased the business from Abner Wyman in 1858 and constructed the factory complex shown in this chromolithograph. After merging with the Gifford ice elevator company, the business relocated to Hudson, New York, in the early twentieth century.

This double house was constructed on Massachusetts Avenue for the families of William Wood and his brother Cyrus, who joined him in managing the adjacent business. It was quite common for nineteenth-century factory owners to build their homes within sight of their business plants.

William T. Wood poses with his family in an 1860s daguerreotype. Note the boldly patterned prints of the boys' outfits.

The Linwood Street icehouse was destroyed in a spectacular fire in 1930. The structures were especially vulnerable to fire because the space between the inner and outer walls was insulted with such flammable matter as sawdust or ground cork. The advent of electric refrigeration had already harkened the demise of the local ice-cutting industry. It persisted for a while longer on northern New England lakes, were there was greater certainty of a harvest each winter.

The blacksmith shop of Thomas Higgins occupied this sturdy brick building constructed in 1864 on Massachusetts Avenue close to present-day Robbins Road. (Society for the Preservation of New England Antiquities.)

Another Arlington blacksmith poses at the anvil in his shop. Some smithies confined their expertise to horse-shoeing. Others worked as carriage builders, or as in this shop, as bicycle repairmen.

Ruben LeBaron, inventor of the pressurized fire whistle, is seen with apprentices in his shop. His wife, Iola, learned the trade here, and in the 1920s she was the only woman to be a licensed master electrician in Massachusetts.

The fire wagon for Hose No. 3 of the Arlington Fire Department is trotted out for this c. 1886 photograph. The wagon was manufactured locally by carriage maker Charles Gott (who was also chief of the fire department). The coming of the automobile would do away with such interdependency between local manufacturing and town services.

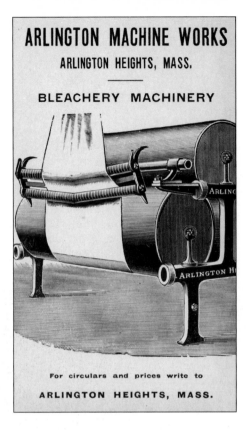

ARLINGTON MACHINE WORKS

ARLINGTON HEIGHTS, MASS.

———

BLEACHERY MACHINERY

For circulars and prices write to

ARLINGTON HEIGHTS, MASS.

Even after the heyday of the mills, other industries proudly attached the Arlington name to their products. This postcard advertises Arthur Birch's machinery business, located on Bow Street at the turn of the century.

ARLINGTON MACHINE WORKS

ARTHUR BIRCH, TREASURER

TEXTILE FINISHING MACHINERY

WORKS ON BOSTON & MAINE R.R.
TELEPHONE · ARLINGTON
TELEGRAMS · WESTERN UNION

CABLE ADDRESS ARBIRCH · BOSTON

This bill head advertises the Arlington Machine Works' proximity to the now-abandoned Boston and Maine Railroad line. This link was vital for the continued presence of industry in Arlington, for it was the only way to effectively move product inland before the era of heavy trucking and superhighways.

A worker leads a two-wheeled horse cart laden with celery from the fields. "Arlington Pure White" celery was particularly famous in the Boston area.

The Henry J. Locke farmhouse (built *c.* 1810 with mansard roof added *c.* 1870) was once located near Massachusetts and Churchill Avenues. The Locke farm was one of the largest in town, but it made little use of the greenhouse methods of production. The house was moved to 35 Bailey Road when the long-coveted land was finally subdivided for residences in the early 1920s.

The Daniel Tappan farm was located at 269 Massachusetts Avenue. The mansard or Second Empire-style house was locally referred to as "French roofed." Local architect/builder James Chase was credited in his obituary for having built "most" of Arlington's buildings of this style.

This view of Franklin Wyman's farm on Lake Street gives an idea of just how extensive Arlington's market "gardens" could be. The Kelwyn Manor neighborhood was developed in these fields starting in 1938. The structure on the left is a standpipe, filled with water for crop irrigation. The smokestack at right was for the boiler supplying steam heat to the greenhouses.

WOMEN FARMERS

A MOMENT FOR THE CAMERA

In the autumn of 1909, the *Boston Herald* ran a photograph essay on the female harvest workers of Arlington's market gardens, most of whom were Italian immigrant women who commuted from Boston's North End by trolley. In spring, they engaged in more informal harvesting—picking dandelion greens for their own consumption from the lawns of the Pleasant Street mansions.

This shot was entitled "Skyscrapers." It depicts the women carrying their empty produce boxes for a morning of picking in the fields.

Scenes such as these so close to the city had already become a novelty by 1909. The original photographs appear to be lost; however, the author's copies made from the yellowed and torn newspaper still manage to convey the personal and very human dimension of a work force that was previously understood only in the abstract.

NOT FRANCE, BUT ARLINGTON

Once filled with produce, the crates were piled in shorter stacks to be carted away from the fields.

Arlington's market gardeners were active in their enterprises—unlike wealthy gentleman farmers—and Franklin Wyman is likely to be among those posing for this *c.* 1915 photograph. That could even be his hat being borrowed by the horse to the left!

Two "putty gunners" are busy at work. This lost occupation in Arlington was once one of the most important to the success of hothouse gardening.

Five

Consolidating Growth: 1900–1915

The early years of the twentieth century saw a continuation of trends that had begun in the 1890s, and most notable among these was the completion of the Civic Block in Arlington Center. In 1913, with great pageantry, the Robbins Memorial Town Hall was dedicated. Unlike its predecessor sixty years earlier, where retail shops occupied the first floor, the new town hall was built to house the functions of local government exclusively. The adjacent Winfield Robbins Memorial Garden was made a focal point of town pride, in contrast to dusty Russell Park, the much-neglected public green space in the center of town. The beautiful structures on the Civic Block gave Arlingtonians every reason to feel pleased with themselves and the growth of their community.

Squire's Garden would be the first major residential subdivision of the new century. These lands of the John P. Squire estate would eventually be developed into a neighborhood of large, two-family homes on small lots, specifically targeted to trolley-taking commuters. Whittemore Park, closer to the Cambridge line, would open for development shortly thereafter. Ironically, what had been recently one of Arlington's most sparsely settled sections would quickly become the most densely populated.

During this time the population soared from 8,600 to over 14,000. Newcomers, including many former city dwellers, lost no time in protesting the "nuisances" created by their older agricultural neighbors. As land values and tax assessments rose, it seemed smarter for the farmers to sell rather than to defend their livelihood in such a fancy "new" town.

The automobile would make its presence quickly felt. The police braced themselves to deal with speed and safety issues raised by the new contraption. The top carriage maker in town abandoned his trade to open the first car repair shop. And many car owners faced the dilemma of living in homes of the latest fashion with no place to garage a motor vehicle (deed covenants of the era frequently prohibited outbuildings, having in mind the "nuisance" of horse barns)— or even to lay a driveway!

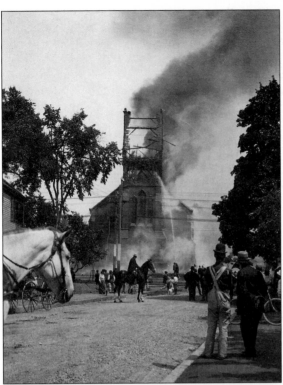

The fire that destroyed the First Baptist Church in 1900 is photographed here looking down Bartlett Avenue. This was the first of the four tall steeples to vanish from the town's skyline. The present church structure of stone was completed in 1903.

Fred M. Chase was the first person in Arlington to own a motor car, the one-cylinder "Locomobile" shown here.

ST. AGNES CHURCH AND RECTORY, ARLINGTON, MASS.

The growing prosperity and influence of Catholics in town was reflected in the enlargement and renovation of St. Agnes Church by Arlington architect Howard B.S. Prescott in 1900. The original tower was enlarged and crowned by a steeple, with an arcaded porch connecting it to a second one. The 1879 rectory, located to the left, was destroyed by fire as this book was nearing completion.

The one-story brick structure with the awnings, today known as Fidelity House, originally housed the Arlington telephone exchange. Note the trolley car making its approach; to its left stands the 1888 St. Agnes Grammar School.

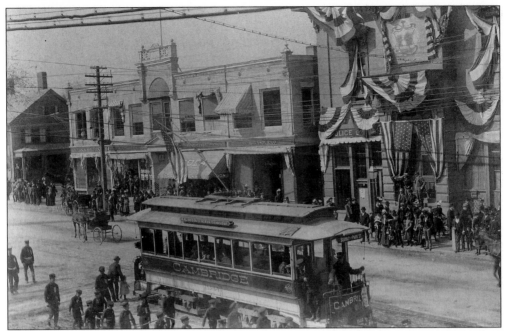

Patriot's Day 1900 found the old town hall, the adjacent Sherburne Block, and even the trolley-car pole appropriately decked out. The Sherburne Block survives, minus its decorative parapet, as the home of DeWolfe Realtors.

This eighteenth-century building at the corner of Massachusetts Avenue and Water Street housed the Russell Grocery, which was famous for the Revolutionary raid in which casks of molasses were left running by the British. The photograph can be dated to 1906 because many windows have been removed for the building's destruction, which made way for the extension of the Associates Block. (Boston Public Library.)

This *c.* 1910 advertising postcard, photographed at the former site of the old Russell Grocery building, reminds us of the importance of local delivery services in the days before private automobiles became common. Large shipments would be carried by train, and businesses such as Wood Bros. handled the leg between the depot and one's home or business.

By 1907, this cluster of Renaissance Revival commercial fronts was completed by the extension of the Associate's Block at left. The storefronts harmonized beautifully with each other, and with Robbins Library, their stylistic counterpart immediately across the street.

The second Cutter School (1864) is seen here after its conversion to apartments at the beginning of the twentieth century. The structure is still in fine condition at 1070–1072 Massachusetts Avenue (minus its distinctive "classroom globe" window in the gable peak). It is known today as the Graycross office building.

The home of Dr. Roy Young at 788 Massachusetts Avenue functioned as a hospital for many years before and after the opening of Symmes. Built in 1901, it was torn down in the early 1960s to restore the green space around the Jason Russell House.

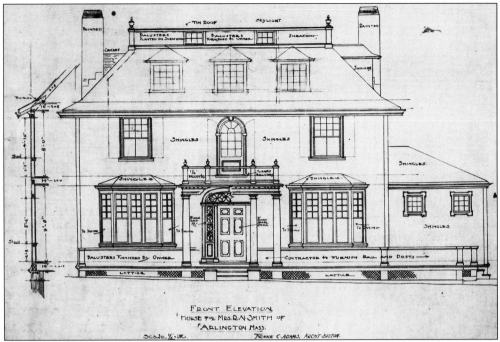

The author's Federal Revival home at 33 Gray Street was built for Mr. and Mrs. Ralph N. Smith in 1902, and features a unique monitor roof with a false balustrade. It was one of the many fine homes by Arlington architects of the era. It was designed by Frank C. Adams, the brother of Mrs. Smith.

The original William E. Parmenter School (1903) was located at the corner of Academy and Irving Streets. It was unique for its era in Arlington because it was constructed of wood. Grades one through four attended this school in classrooms of fifty students each. Designed by Jason Street architect H.B.S. Prescott, it boasted "a hygienic drinking fountain and a footwarmer in the central hall."

Increased street and railroad traffic led to the elimination of several grade crossings. This 1900 view shows the Brattle Street depot at the left. Above the handsome granite retaining wall sits a typical nineteenth-century laborer's home. It once survived a roof fire from the sparks of a passing train, but eventually became vulnerable to rising land values and was razed in 1996 to make way for a new duplex.

Donnelly Advertising's billboards once adorned Massachusetts Avenue. This is a 1915 view of the edge of the Heights, looking into East Lexington.

Saint Anne's Chapel, Arlington Heights, Massachusetts

Saint Anne's Chapel is one of Arlington's architectural jewels, designed by Ralph Adams Cram. It is discreetly located on Claremont Avenue. It was built in 1915, and served the worship needs of the order of Episcopal nuns who founded an orphanage there.

The Convent Chapel of Saint Anne, Arlington Heights, Massachusetts

This view of the medieval-style interior of the chapel shows but one breathtaking aspect of the decoration of the sanctuary. The work of the sisters changed over the years and led them to establish St. Anne's School on the campus of the former orphanage. It is currently a residential treatment facility for girls and is named for its founder, Sister Germaine Lawrence.

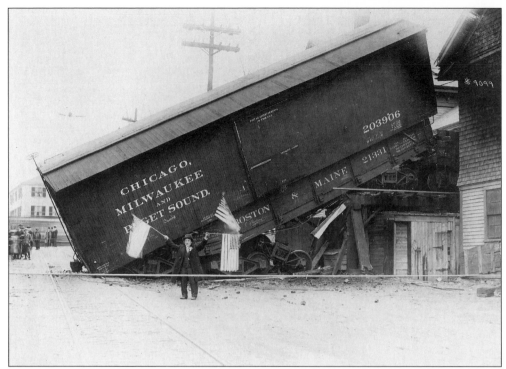

This patriotic eccentric looks a bit like Charlie Chaplin! He is dwarfed by the spectacular box-car pileup at Peirce and Winn's coal yard in 1903. The site is Mystic Street (on its previous traffic alignment) looking toward Massachusetts Avenue.

Workers sweep away debris from an explosion at the Arlington Gas Light office in 1913. It was perhaps not the best advertisement for the safety of the company's product! This block stood where the drive-up window and parking lot of the Cambridge Savings Bank are located today.

The Civil War monument is all that can be recognized today from this postcard view. The Central Fire Station with its tower had overwhelmed the little memorial park by 1928, and the commercial growth of Arlington Center would soon vastly alter the streetscape of old Broadway.

Alewife Brook was rip-rapped (channeled) around 1910 to end the pollution and flooding problems that had plagued northeast Arlington for decades. A corner of St. Paul's Catholic Cemetery is in the right foreground; to the rear is the footbridge that today leads from the Alewife Brook Parkway to the Hendersonville neighborhood.

This squad of bowler-hatted gents looks more like a group of raiders than a team. Note the old-fashioned curve of the hockey sticks.

A turn-of-the-century hockey team warms up for play atop Spy Pond.

"Skateboating" was a picturesque pastime for this Spy Pond trio in the early years of this century. Note the Linwood Street icehouse to the right. The slope-roofed extension on the facade housed the conveyor, or "endless" belt, that transported the ice blocks from the lake to the storage area.

Dorothy Homer (Chamberlain) serves up a ball on the courts of the Arlington Lawn Tennis Club, which was located off Pleasant Street.

In bloomers and neckties, the Arlington High School Girls Basketball Team of 1909 lines up

for this panoramic shot.

For over a dozen years into this century, Town Meeting was held in the second-floor auditorium of the old town hall. Shown here are the refurbishments for its final legislative use, featuring the addition of electric lighting. The old chandeliers were kept in place and operating because gas would remain a reliable and necessary source of back-up illumination for several years to come.

In a scene from the Arlington Pageant to celebrate the new town hall, members of The Arlington Historical Society portray spectators at the 1867 celebration of the town's name change from West Cambridge to Arlington. Many of the older members had attended the original event!

The *Menotomy Indian Hunter,* one of Cyrus Dallin's finest works, stands at the head of the waterfall in the Winfield Robbins Memorial Garden, adjacent to town hall. The figure is posed with one hand cupped for refreshment, the other firmly clutching the bow to promptly resume the pheasant hunt.

Other significant sculptures by Cyrus Dallin are located at the corners of the base of the town hall flagpole. Shown here, from the left, are a Puritan Divine, a Puritan mother reading to her child, and an Indian squaw. A Minuteman (facing the former Universalist church to the rear) completes the grouping. Liberty, Honesty, Obedience, and Patriotism are the four virtues inscribed.

Two chickens peck for worms on the newly cleared site for the high school on Massachusetts Avenue in 1913. The background buildings on the right belong to the Arlington Gas Light Company (the DPW yard today). The much-protested gas holding tank was also being built that year, and would be an eyesore in town until it was dismantled in 1976.

With the just-dedicated town hall in the background, the last class to study ancient Greek at Arlington High School poses near the entrance to the old school in 1913. The dead language was once a requirement for those who pursued the prestigious "classical course" diploma as preparation for college.

Six
The Mature Suburb: 1916–1950

In the years between the two world wars, the scales of development finally tipped away from agriculture in favor of housing. This switch can be measured by the number of listings under "Market Gardens" in the Arlington directories. There were forty in 1910, but only twenty-seven in 1920, and thirteen in 1930. By 1940 only three were listed. It was not just that a great number of market gardens had ceased operation, but that most of the larger farm holdings (30 to 50 acres) were subdivided in the 1920s and 1930s. The dramatic shift from a preponderance of open land to one of homes with families placed an enormous strain on town resources. Schools reached capacity almost as fast as they could be built. Soon large apartment blocks began to sprout along Massachusetts Avenue, and it seemed as if the lines between city and suburb would be blurred before there was time to react.

During this era, changes in the social makeup of the town also accelerated. With the building of St. Jerome's in 1938, church structures for Roman Catholics surpassed those of any single denomination in Arlington. And although the town still voted Republican right through the Depression, the Democratic Party would soon start to carry Arlington in state and national elections—and retain predominance for the rest of the century.

Clubs continued to thrive, but changed their focus as new forms of entertainment appeared. Dances, minstrel shows, and sailing regattas lost their appeal as the Arlington Boat Club membership grew older. Its property was eventually sold to the Middlesex Sportsmen's Association in 1920. Vaudeville and silent features became the rage at the Regent Theatre, and soon after, "talking pictures" gained popularity at the elegant Capitol movie house.

Immediately after World War II, Arlington's population was approximately 44,000—roughly what it has been in recent years. But the baby boom and a last gasp of extensive residential construction yet to come meant that the town had at least a dozen years to go before hitting its population peak. The 1940s drew to a close with the specter of the state running a multi-lane expressway through northeast Arlington. A now fully mature suburb had to contend with environmental and quality-of-life issues remarkably similar to many facing it today.

This notice board at the corner of Pleasant Street and Massachusetts Avenue was used by the Red Cross during World War I to post news from the front and other information in the days before radio. After the Armistice, it was happily converted to cheer the return of Arlingtonians who had served in the military.

A grand welcome-home celebration was held on June 19, 1919, for the "doughboys" and sailors returning from the Great War in Europe. This group is posing near the old fountain by the First Parish Unitarian Church.

Fred M. Chase was intrepid, to say the least. The first automobile owner in town also became the first local to purchase an airplane in 1919. As the photographer of the 1897 pictures taken from the Unitarian church steeple, his thirst for aerial views was an established fact in town.

A pair of biplanes has been pasted into this c. 1918 novelty photo postcard scene. Artists would frequently add interest to these images by inserting people, cars, boats—even flags on bare poles.

Storefronts obscure the ground floor of the Jonathan Marsh Dexter house, an historic site where the nation's first children's library was founded in 1837. It was shamefully destroyed in 1974 for the construction of a drive-up window at the old Arlington Five Cents Savings Bank. It was not entirely uncommon to see both horse-drawn and motor-driven transportation in Arlington well into the 1930s.

This steam engine has just left Arlington Center on its way to Boston in this *c.* 1920 view of the present-day Minuteman Bikeway.

A bygone symbol of Arlington's welfare and safety was the old fire tower bell, located on Pond Lane behind Arlington's first triple-decker apartment complex, The Florence.

This 1926 picture shows the test run of a new Fordson Tractor, which is plowing snow on Mystic Street. The Arlington Steam Laundry building is to the rear.

The nursing staff poses c. 1920 at the entrance of what was originally designated the Symmes Building of Arlington Hospital. Endowed by a bequest from Stephen Symmes in 1901, the hospital did not go up until 1909. Fund-raising for the purchase of equipment continued until its first patient could be admitted in 1912.

The admitting office and switchboard shared quarters at Symmes Arlington Hospital c. 1920. To recognize the importance of the medical facility to patients from Lexington, the name was shortened to its present "Symmes Hospital" about thirty years later.

The 1924 graduating class of the Symmes Arlington Training School for Nurses is shown here. All the nearsighted students have been clustered together for this portrait, perhaps due to the photographer's lighting requirements. The school was in operation until 1948.

The basement of the Symmes Hospital nurses' residence was staffed by a maid and decorated to serve as a formal dining room. It is said that in the early years of the Symmes nursing school, etiquette lessons were included to train the young women for possible private duty and companionship assignments in upper-class homes.

Travelers heading down Pleasant Street toward Winchester were confronted with this sight at Massachusetts Avenue instead of the wide and straight four-way intersection that is there today. The cupola of the old West Cambridge Town House had been damaged by lightning in this August 1923 photograph and was ordered to undergo immediate removal.

Its facade worn down to the bare brick, the old West Cambridge Town House was torn down altogether in 1960 for the realignment of Mystic Street. The tiny park with Uncle Sam's statue occupies a portion of this site adjacent to the old Arlington National Bank.

The Neoclassical Masonic Temple was built at the head of Maple Street on Academy in 1924. It occupies the site of the Cotting High School.

WATER TOWER, ARLINGTON HEIGHTS, MASSACHUSETTS   6773

Inspired by their visit to Greece, the Robbins sisters donated this temple-form standpipe at Park Circle. Designed by Arlington architect Frederick E. Low, the nearly 2-million-gallon tank was completed for nearly $2 million in 1924. Visitors could enjoy a breathtaking panoramic view of the Boston basin to the New Hampshire hills from its observation gallery.

Arlington Center is shown looking east in the 1930s. Note the original Stop & Shop on the left. Diagonal, front-in street parking was possible because there was no need for bus stops; the trolley ran down the center of Massachusetts Avenue.

Please Call
Street
City
Telephone

In the days before people routinely discarded their older clothing, businesses such as the Arlington Dye Works at 91 Mystic Street were much in demand to make fashions fresh and new. The building has most recently housed Media One's cable television offices and studios.

The streetscape of the Arlington Heights commercial district has changed little since this 1930s postcard view was produced. However, the buildings have lost some of their major decorative elements, such as the roof balustrade above Menotomy Pharmacy, and the fanlight decoration on the Brigham's facade.

In the 1930 Arlington Pageant celebrating the tercentenary of the Massachusetts Bay Colony, Judge John Gaylord Brackett (son of the former governor) depicted Abraham Lincoln, and Michael Manning (in blackface and body stocking) played the slave, in a tableau based on the well-known *Emancipation* statute. A copy of this sculpture, viewed as controversial by some, stands in Boston's Park Square.

After the great 1938 hurricane compromised the steeple of the Universalist church, it was replaced by the beautiful cupola shown here. Following the merger of this denomination with the Unitarians in the 1960s, the building became home to St. Athanasius the Great Greek Orthodox parish. It is thus the oldest continuous-use religious structure standing in Arlington.

Amateur cameras, such as the Kodak Box Brownie that an Arlington Heights dad is using here, created a paradox where historical images are concerned. They resulted in a proliferation of everyday scenes following World War I; however, these tended to be pasted in private albums and eventually discarded by future generations rather than being ceremoniously presented to friends and collecting organizations as earlier images had been.

What's perhaps most remarkable about this snapshot of "Sis" posing by—of all things—the clothesline, is how it represents Arlington's final shift towards middle-class suburbia. No longer a town of "servants and the served," its population continued to swell with new housing in the 1930s for city-dwellers seeking their own bit of green backyard.

Many Arlington men were employed in the Works Projects Administration (WPA) program during the Great Depression. In this scene, the Mill Brook is being rip-rapped—channeled between man-made walls.

The Arlington Branch of the American Red Cross at Boston was reactivated in 1941. Here a volunteer delivers blood plasma to a capped-and-caped nurse at Symmes Arlington Hospital, while her partner sits tight in her genuine wood-paneled Plymouth "beach wagon."

"An Aluminum Shower for Uncle Sam and Lady Liberty," was how the *Advocate* described this 1941 metal drive that collected two tons of aluminum for the war effort. The aluminum came mostly in the form of old pots and pans, but one anonymous patriot contributed a set of aluminum-mounted false teeth!

The Arlington Boat Club sold its property to the Middlesex Sportsman's Association in 1920, and that group transferred ownership to the Arlington Boys Club in 1943. As can be seen in this photograph taken behind the old clubhouse, the swimming pool was an outdoor affair.

This 1948 aerial view of the town center is useful to understand the relative proximity of several vanished structures in the lower left quadrant: the Unitarian church, the old town hall, the train depot, and the railroad spur leading to the Peirce and Winn coal sheds and hardware store on Mystic Street.

James O. Holt stands in front of the Pleasant Street market during its last week of operation in 1948, shortly before his death. His advanced age and the coming of the supermarket era made the closing a wise choice for Holt. He had risen from store clerk in the late nineteenth century to the owner of two contiguous groceries located where the drive-up entrance to the Cambridge Savings Bank exists today.

When first converted to banking use around 1920, the Renaissance Revival-style Studio Building was given a sculpted concrete facade that eliminated its harmony with the Associates Block next door. Its later exterior remodeling settled on a comparatively insipid neither-Greek-nor-Colonial-Revival design. It most recently became a BankBoston branch.

Buttrick's original retail ice cream stand to the rear of its 30 Mill Street plant was a popular gathering spot, especially for high schoolers, as was the larger restaurant built adjacent to it. Brigham's moved its corporate headquarters to the Buttrick site after acquisition of the dairy in the late 1960s, and it continues to operate the restaurant there.

The Cold War was on when the Knights of Columbus sponsored this Patriot's Day parade float in the early 1950s. A Soviet soldier (looking more like a Cossack guard from the days of the Czar) is depicted repressing religious freedom. Meanwhile, Uncle Sam (looking more like the Abominable Snowman) is pointing out the virtues of Lady Liberty.

This seemingly ordinary view, looking northeast at Park Circle around 1950, wonderfully captures the transition of Arlington's past and present. Dutch Colonial homes of the 1930s share the left two-thirds of this image with a Boston Elevated Railway bus waiting to carry commuters to the then-nearest subway at Harvard Square. The former Outlook spa hotel, at right, has been converted to a nursing home, and finally would come under the wrecking ball in the 1980s for another cluster of suburban dwellings.

Epilogue

Although it might have escaped the reader's notice, the final chapter of this book was somewhat shorter than the others. Ironically, only the chronological chapter covering the earliest years of photography had a lower ratio of pictures-to-years-covered than this one. Obviously, it is not the case that there were fewer photographs produced in this period, but rather that fewer were believed to be worthy of collection. The result of this thinking is that gaps have developed in local archival holdings. Vital tools for immediately visualizing the everyday past simply haven't become available.

The trend is not likely to change without conscious intervention on the part of all who care about developing a comprehensive record of every era through images. Modern digital processes in newspaper production often mean that an actual original photograph is never created, just the fragile newspaper version. Furthermore, the consolidated editorial offices of suburban newspaper chains no longer routinely keep local photograph files in an accessible fashion. Family members disperse across the country, and those who come upon a late relative's scrapbook containing images of a town they don't really know or care about will often discard the priceless item as worthless.

Arlington will celebrate its 200th anniversary as an independent town in the year 2007. The challenge of the next decade is to actively gather, identify, and preserve historic images through donation to the archives of The Arlington Historical Society—be they postcards from the 1960s, or snapshots of places and events as varied as those presented in this volume.

Let us assure that the record of the events, people, and places that were important in our lives can be understood and appreciated by the generations to follow.

Richard A. Duffy
Arlington, Massachusetts
June 9, 1997

Acknowledgments

I gratefully acknowledge the cooperation and support I received from many individuals in the course of producing *Arlington*.

Special thanks are owed to Patricia C. Fitzmaurice, executive trustee of The Old Schwamb Mill, for her particular interest in this work—shown in ways ranging from running photographic errands, to our many valuable and mirthful conversations on a wide range of historical topics.

Members of The Arlington Historical Society have been enthusiastic supporters, especially my fellow officers and directors. William H. Mahoney generously loaned the best images from his personal collection. Tina Dorr kept tabs on me by day, just as Irene Capes made sure I wasn't freezing in the archives by night. Former Registrar Vivian Wood's years of dedication deserve special praise here. The Smith Museum's Centennial Exhibit designer, Lisa Ann Welter, kindly volunteered to help me re-file images, earning untold thanks. John L. Worden III has been particularly encouraging of my writings from the very beginning.

The Adult Services Librarians at Robbins Library are delightful—each and every one. The exceptional cooperation I have received from Jennifer DeRemer is deeply appreciated, as is the organizational legacy of former staff member Deb Ervin.

In addition to discovering wonderful images on my expanded search, I discovered wonderful caretakers of these treasures (or got to better appreciate the ones I already knew): Lorna Condon and Ann Clifford (Society for the Preservation of New England Antiquities); Catharina Slautterback and Sally Pierce (Boston Athenæum); Julie Corwin (Symmes Hospital); Aaron Schmidt (Boston Public Library); and Pat Donoghue and Madeleine Mullin (Harvard University).

Personal thanks to my parents for loan of the Antiguan "writer's garret." To my niece, Hilary Hughes, who stepped in at a critical phase to serve as my production assistant. To Mary Trvalik for her inspiration. To Jamie Carter, my editor at Arcadia Publishing, who kept me on-track *and* laughing. But most of all to José Rodríguez, whose many helpful suggestions, editing, support, and endless listening were instrumental in the success of my work.

Reproduction permission fees
were provided by the Lorinda "Lindy" Roberts Memorial Fund
at The Arlington Historical Society.